# WOMEN
## can be so ANNOYI

But you gotta love 'em

by
Steve Hurt

Playground
PUBLISHING

Published by Playground Publishing

Published by:
Playground Publishing
P.O. Box 125, Portsmouth
Hampshire  PO1 4PP
Tel: 01705 819162
Fax: 01705 734814

ISBN:  0-9535987-1-3

Cartoons by Ford
Cartoons in the gallery by Silvey Jex Partnership
Limericks by Liz Garrad
Printed In UK

# Why can't women be as nice as men?

Women aren't nice like men, that is clear
   they don't watch enough sport or drink beer
      they like a good cry and I just can't see why
         no, I can't understand them I fear.

Once a month they get rude and aggressive
   and for what?  it's a mystery to me
      they stamp and they shout
         and they throw things  about
            but they'll never admit PMT

They spend hours restyling their hair
   spend cash like they don't have a care
      they buy millions of clothes
         and that's why I suppose
            they say they've got nothing to wear

They don't like it if they're left alone
   they gossip for hours on the phone
      and though every things gleaming
         they're obsessed with the cleaning
            yes for Britain these women could moan

They hate football, can't understand cricket
   the joys of these games are above 'em
      Women can be so annoying
         but for all that – *you just gotta love 'em!*

3

# Women's mothering instincts

Now wrap up warm it's cold outside, and have you got your keys?
That's it, and a clean hanky dear - in case you have to sneeze.
Now let me see your handies - are they really nice and clean?
and in case you're stuck in traffic - tell me dear - now have you been?
Play nicely with the others - don't be bossy, understand?
and if you need some typing done - ask nicely - don't demand
That's it now - off you go dear - with a great big smile for me
and hurry home this evening 'cause there's toast and jam for tea!!

# Why do women always want to change us?

I think you need some training, to do just what I say
so when we go out shopping, and I say now pay – you pay
Your coat is awfully smelly, it could almost make me wretch
and when it comes to presents, well you need to learn to fetch
Obedience classes are the thing, they'll sort you out a bit
get in the car, it's not too far, yes here we are – now sit.

# No please don't — OK I love you, here I said it!

I had Harold frozen, until they
find a cure for cold-heartedness

You're hardly the warmest of husbands it's true
there's just no affection whatever I do
you don't talk to me or laugh very much
and I just can't make you respond to my touch
so I'm having you frozen - yes every last part
now the rest of your body is as cold as your heart!

# There's just no pleasing women!

Flowers?! – Chocolate?! – Who says I want flowers and chocolate?! – What have you been up to? – What are you feeling guilty about?

Chocolates – oh yeah so what have you done
have you been unfaithful or had too much fun
you know I hate chocolates – oh shut up and be quiet
you ruined my will power and also my diet
Flowers – oh now what – and please why today?
are you going to confess – have you something to say?
I'm so easy to please – that's so easy to see
Me – give me strength – they're a mystery to me

# I'm not going, I have nothing to wear!

It's really not fair I don't know what to wear
Oh stop laughing you're always so mean
Women can be so snide and I do have my pride
I can't wear an outfit they've seen
Don't stand there and shout, no please help me out
and find something that I've never worn
Yes – I think you're quite right – these curtains are bright
but darling – do they make me look drawn?

Just picture this..... You have been ready for almost an hour. You have worked out the route, warmed up the car, and are beginning to perspire in your overcoat. To be on time, you should have left twenty minutes ago, not allowing for the traffic or parking. So with a very calm voice, so as not to ruin the evening, you say, "Come on darling, we're going to be late." Then you hear those dreaded words uttered from the bedroom, "I'm not going – I have nothing to wear!" Then you go completely numb, and just sit and wonder why this has to happen to you every single time...

# Women's No. 1 Obsession.

You just don't seem to get it
you just don't understand
it really really cheers me up
by spending seven grand
I know we didn't need it
that means sod all to me
There's really nothing like
a bit of retail therapy
as since you're sending me away
I've bought new clothes as well
so have a heart, I must look smart, in my padded cell

# Women drivers

Women drivers - Bless 'em - They are so sweet and thoughtful.  I wonder if we could ever be as considerate as women drivers!

I had a little accident today so don't be mad
I was driving and I saw this little boy and he looked sad
his ball had rolled in to the road - so I stopped for him you see
I wonder if the Motor way's the safest place to be
I should have just kept driving - but it's just my rotten luck
Pardon darling - where's the car? - It's parked beneath a truck!

# Women in the passenger seat

.........Mind that bicycle .......slow down.......is this the right way?...... look out for....

Don't drive too near the pavement, mind that woman - mind that child
the trouble is with blokes in cars, it tends to send them wild
Mind that poor old pensioner, look out a motorbike
you put a chap behind the wheel, he'll do just what he like
I worry when I ride with you, that I'll get home alive
now - sweetie start the car, because we're still parked on the drive

# Why are women never satisfied.....

You give a woman the world, and she wants the universe. You give her the universe, and she'll moan about how long she had to wait for it, or how you presented it to her. Her response would probably be: "So and so got it before she even desired it." Is this idea of the grass being greener over the other side, so deeply rooted in their mind that they will never be satisfied? or are we men taking this obsession of women too personally, looking upon it as a series of fail marks for our efforts?

# Can women survive without gossip?

Before we start, I'm sorry to report that Julie has resigned – she has some personal problems – I expect it's something to do with the rumours about her husband and his secretary – not to mention that amazing story.......

The Committee for the Abolition of Gossip

I bumped into Esmerelda at the shops the other day
her recent nose job didn't go too well, I have to say
and she's looking quite well rounded – so I couldn't mention that
it doesn't do to say, "Well frankly darling – you look FAT!"
and her hubby has lost interest – if you follow what I mean
but when the Au Pair's there – then his expression's much more keen
so I'd say that in conclusion, she's not happy on the whole
but of course – it's confidential dear – so please don't tell a soul.

# Some women just don't bother..

Oh please come on darling – lets have an early night
you know you love my hairy legs – adore my cellulite
you appreciate my beard and thankful that you do
and the fact I never bathe – I think you like that too
we make a perfect couple when all is done and said
but I'm tempted to leave – cause I simply can't breathe
with this bag that you've put on my head.

# Why are women obsessed about cleaning?

Why are women obsessed about cleaning?
The house just looks perfect to me
But she gets in a fluster
she's waving a duster
at dirt that I just cannot see.
She's buzzing about with the vacuum
and I can't hear the match for the din
Well I've heard enough about dust motes and fluff
So I'll just go and sit in the bin!!

# Women — You can't live with them....

# .......you can't live with them!

What's the matter, you look happy - are you listening to me Steven
'cause what I do - you'll find it's true - I don't get mad - just even.

# Women do not nag!!

We are so ungrateful accusing our kind and considerate women of nagging, when all the time they are merely trying to help us...

You see sweetheart – I'm not nagging
no I'm merely helping you
to recognise the little things you really need to do
I'm trying to instil in you some knowledge for my part
learning how to pick up empty cans would be a start
it will help you in the future
give you purpose – give you hope
and if we get a miracle – you might start using soap!!

We should therefore for our part respond to the kind gestures and submit full-heartedly, and really believe that women do not nag...

Darling you say you're not nagging
if I only believed that was true
You always say that it's your little way
of pointing out things I should do
So I'll try to observe your instructions
If I don't you'll just stand there and gloat
But in future my dear, could you not bend my ear
I'd prefer if you left me a note.

# Women do not nag!!

It is quite obvious that occasionally men and women experience problems in communications which can only be put down to semantics. Just as we understand the word selfish, but we cannot comprehend how the word could possibly be related to us. Women also fully understand the word Nagging, but find it hard to associate it with their attempt to actually communicate with us.

# Where do women get the idea we don't understand them?

Yeah...yeah....Very funny! This joke about us not understanding women, is getting a little thin, so I intend to stop it once and for all by revealing the truth....You see, we do understand women very well, but are too clever to let on, because if we do, then we have to respond to their every whim, mood and desire. Isn't it easier for us to just say, "Sorry luv, I just don't understand women", and be let off the hook scot-free?

# Why can't women leave our egos alone?

Would you kick a man while he's down?....Women do! Every time we try to get up and begin to rebuild our confidence, they attack again.   Their gun is always loaded and ready to fire.  Loaded with those spiteful comments, aimed straight at the most sensitive and fragile part of us........our ego. Comments like "Never mind you did your best" or "still....you've got a lovely personality instead" Do they not realise that comments like these leave a deep scar, and take years to heal?

# Sorry luv, I've got a headache!

Women just don't understand the repercussions of uttering those dreaded words; particularly after the guy's reluctant endeavour to be clean and presentable. ..And when you show disappointment they say:

Darling don't be selfish – I'm tired and want to sleep
Oh wipe that daft look off your face- it's enough to make me weep
Oh don't start going on – it's really such a bore
if you want to use some energy – then wash the kitchen floor

# Can you do it NOW please?

What's the panic, dear? – Fire? – burst pipe? – What...

Just this picture – I want you to put it up NOW, please

Why do women always insist on having those dreaded odd jobs done at the least convenient times. ...And how is it that they always manage to have a string of them up their sleeves, to pull out at will, and nag about, just to annoy you.

Oh you want it doing now
I really should have known
I was only in the bath
I really shouldn't moan
You know your every little whim
is my hearts desire
when I heard you shout
I just jumped out
I thought you were on fire!!

# "I'd like you to come shopping with me today, dear"

No please – don't take me to the shops
It really isn't fair
I'll just have to hold your handbag
and stand by the underwear
You'll drag me round and round the town
Until I'm fit to burst
And at closing time, you'll buy a dress
in the shop we went to first

# "I'd like you to come shopping with me today, dear"

Oh darling please try smiling
oh you just look such a mess
I've never seen such fuss because I want to buy a dress
we haven't been here all that long
I don't know what you mean
if you count it in hours
well it's only seventeen
now stand up straight
give me a little kiss
then come in here and tell me
do I look fat in this?

My therapist calls my life threatening phobia of Saturdays, "Saturday Fever"! The symptoms; cold sweat, dry mouth and shivers appear every time I hear the word Saturdays. Images of loads of shops, filled with women's clothes, and contented women dragging their men around, haunts me. I keep hearing the unbearable phrase, "I like you to come shopping with me today, dear". Then I wake up screaming, not again, not again....

# PMT?....Who's got PMT?....

Oh no – Oh my Gawd lets take cover
she's got that mad look on her face
I don't care what she says
every twenty eight days
she starts throwing her weight round the place
the kids cover and hide out in corners
the dog's packed his bowl and is leaving
and it seems every time, that my only crime
is I'm here – I'm alive and I'm breathing!

# Why is it *so* important to notice those tiny changes?

I'm terrified of coming home
In case something has changed
Her make up or her hair
or something in that range
I wish she didn't ask me
I don't notice things, it's true
I'd like to say meet me half way
At least give me a clue.

# Isn't it fun to share interests?!

And one and two and three and four
now lift those legs high off the floor
let's tighten up those flabby tums
let's shake those lovely lycra bums
come on Eric shake your bits
we'll teach you how to do the splits
Oh there's your friends – see how they grin
perhaps you'd like to ask them in
then they like you, can work real hard
and wear a nice pink leotard.

# We can't eat – I'm on a diet.

I don't believe it! I've lost another ½ Ounce!

If we stick to this lot for a month, we're allowed half a cream cake!

DOG·O·DIET
ONLY ONE CALORIE

CALORIE COUNT

I'm really sick of lettuce
It doesn't taste that nice
I'd much prefer a curry
with lots and lots of rice
But we have to watch your figure
And that's why we eat this stuff
Well watch your figure on your own
ME – I've seen enough

# The word 'gullible' has been omitted from the dictionary!

I am not saying that all women are gullible, but those few who are make up for the rest of them. They fall for the same old tricks that men have been dishing out for centuries, over and over again.

......Or is it possible that they are not really gullible, and that they are just humouring us, and protecting us and our ego in our attempt to be clever and our quest to be better than them.

# Who is exploiting women?

I simply don't agree with your proposition that women are being exploited or being treated in anyway differently to men.

IN THIS MONTH'S MACHO magazine

MAJOR INTERVIEW WITH TOP MODEL

"IT'S JUST A JOB - SOMEONE HAS TO DO IT"

"I WANT TO BE TREATED AS A FELLOW HUMAN BEING - NOT A SEX OBJECT"

M.P.

LATEST

WOMAN SACKED FOR REFUSING TO CONTINUE WEARING SKIMPY TOPS TO SUE MALE BOSS

It's such a load of rubbish – girls are never used to sell
by being just half dressed – of course you know that very well
we don't put them on calendars or drape them over cars
or make them give out leaflets dressed in tiny lacy bras
they're not clothed in next to nothing with a view to tantalise
I don't know where you heard that 'cause to me it's a surprise

# Titles available

From Playground Publishing

**Men can be such idiots,
but you gotta love 'em**
Book plus free Wonderdisk
@ £4.99  (Free postage)
(The Idiotometer &
When he says...he means...)
ISBN 0-9535987-0-5

**Women can be so annoying,
but you gotta love 'em**
Book plus free Wonderdisk
@ £4.99 (Free postage)
(Women-troubleshooting &
When she says.. she means...)
ISBN 0-9535987-1-3

Send your order together with a cheque or postal order payable to
Playground Publishing, PO Box 125, Portsmouth PO1 4PP

If you wish your purchase to be sent directly to someone else
(e.g.: Birthday / Christmas / Wedding / Valentine gift), simply send
your order with your personal message, or card if desired.
We will be pleased to send your gift directly to your chosen recipient.

**Playground**
PUBLISHING